Basic Stairbuilding